MW00963718

MAKING DIVERSITY MEANINGFUL IN THE BOARDROOM

John Carver and
Miriam Mayhew Carver

Jossey-Bass Publishers
San Francisco

Manufactured in the United States of America.

Policy Governance℠ is a service mark of John Carver.

Jossey-Bass Web address: http://www.josseybass.com

Library of Congress Cataloging-in-Publication Data

Carver, John.
    Making diversity meaningful in the boardroom / John Carver and Miriam Mayhew Carver — 1st ed.
      p. cm. — (CarverGuide ; 9)
    ISBN 0-7879-0835-5 (pbk.)
    1. Directors of corporations. 2. Diversity in the workplace.
I. Carver, Miriam Mayhew. II. Title. III. Series: Carver, John.
The CarverGuide series on effective board governance ; 9.
HD2745.C3724 1997
658.4'22—dc21   97-4566

PB Printing   10 9 8 7 6 5 4 3 2 1   FIRST EDITION

Social pressures in recent years have caused many boards to re-examine their commitment to diversity. We think boards inherit an obligation to diversity quite naturally by the very nature of governance. The people on whose behalf boards govern (the ownership concept in Policy Governance) have the right to expect it of them. But what does diversity actually mean in the governance context? Ju.. r what kind of diversity should boards pursue?

Since a governing board is the owner–representative body, gender, racial, religious, and geographic diversity in the ownership can, within limits, be paralleled in board membership. Having women, Blacks, Hispanics, people with disabilities, teens, or environmentalists on the board can indeed enhance true diversity if they enrich board sensitivity to the wishes of its ownership.

But the tendency toward tokenism often burdens these "special" board members with the daunting task of representing everyone with whom they share whatever characteristic that identifies them. That is, women find themselves in the absurd and impossible position of having to "speak for women," as if members of this group do not disagree among themselves. Hispanics have to ignore the rich differences in opinion and culture in their heritage in order to give a "Hispanic point of view." This form of tokenism is merely a cosmetic solution to the important need to govern in a manner that includes the diversity of ownership. Tokenism is but a cheap substitute for finding true diversity and integrating it into governance decision making.

Due to the very nature of governance, there is a moral imperative for diversity in board life. But this imperative does not derive from some abstract commitment to humanity, nor from a politically correct need to have the proper appearance. It springs from the simple fact that responsible action is impossible unless the diversity present in the ownership is integrated into governance. Owners own them (though often in a moral more than a legal sense), and boards represent them. Unless "represent" embraces the range of owner diversity, something is amiss. Hence, we are unable to separate the issue of diversity in the boardroom from the issue of ownership.

In this CarverGuide, we discuss ways that boards can integrate diversity into their group. First, we explore the meaning of ownership and the board's relationship to ownership diversity. Next, we look at ways to ensure that the board is acting on the full ownership's behalf and ways for a board to connect itself properly to that ownership. Then we will suggest ways to gather intelligence from persons outside the boardroom. Finally, we will offer a guide to promoting and handling dissent in the boardroom so that diverse voices can flourish.

Ownership: Whose Diversity Is at Stake?

Very few nonprofit or public boards govern on their own behalf. Ordinarily, boards exercise their authority as a kind of stewardship on behalf of others. In other words, there is some population that, at least in a moral sense if not a legal one, "owns" the organization.

Owners—even if unorganized, unrecognized, and often undefined—constitute the primary object of board allegiance and its source of moral authority. The board-ownership relationship is the essential, defining relationship of a board. Board members stand in for the ownership, operating on its behalf. The board can be seen as a microcosm of the ownership, a workable subpart of an awkwardly large group. It is therefore important to identify the ownership group.

The diversity relevant to board composition and conduct is the diversity of the owners, not the diversity of consumers, of staff, or of other groups. It is not that diversity in these other groups is ignored by the board, just that the board does not represent them.

So, let's be clear about who the owners are not. The concept of ownership is narrower than the concept of *stakeholder,* a term that includes all parties who have an interest in the organization. Stakeholders can be staff, vendors, neighbors, service recipients, and others, as well as those we are calling owners.

The concept of ownership is different from and usually broader than the concept of customership. Confounding the two yields another source of confusion for many boards when they state their accountability in terms of the organization's consumers. While there is no doubt that consumers should have the right to expect to get what they should from the organization, and as such are a very important group, *it is the board that decides who the consumers are, and what results they should get.*

The concept of ownership is also not to be confounded with that of funders. Funders, we need hardly remind you, are bodies to whom a great deal of deference is due, but it is useful to view them as important bulk purchasers, because such a formulation allows boards to see that clearly identifying purchasers does not settle the question of ownership.

In some instances, who the owners are is clear. Most people would agree, we think, that the ownership of a school board is the population of its district (which includes but is not limited to its consumers). The ownership of a city council is the citizenry of the municipality. And the ownership of a trade association is its membership. But the ownership for many nonprofits is often an amorphous general public.

Before we look at how a board can be constituted in a way mindful of its owners' diversity, it is important to note some concerns. There are, in fact, sober judgments to be made regarding what characteristics to reflect and what not to reflect. The task of governance is not for everyone, any more than is any other important role. Board members should possess an atypical propensity and skill for visioning, for seeing the underlying values, and for what we might crudely call big thinking. Illustrating our point at the opposite end of the spectrum, no one argues that a board should have members in proportion to the number of criminals or the severely psychotic in the ownership. In other words, there are quite a few portions of owner diversity that a board need not reflect.

But by what principle do we distinguish the diversity to be pursued from that which need not be? We are unaware of any concepts that directly address this question, meaning that boards and those who appoint boards are thrown back on their best judgment. We do not offer a solution for the dilemma here, but we do point out that a headlong, unthinking thrust toward the politically correct might give insufficient recognition of this matter.

Many boards are tempted to make themselves very large as a way of becoming a likeness of the ownership. However, there is no way that a board can be constituted so that it represents *all* diversity present in the ownership. The entire range of diversity can be accommodated only by swelling the board to an unmanageable size. Consider the extreme: a public or nonprofit board might represent a community of, say, 150,000. Absolute representation of the diversity in such a population would call for putting 150,000 on the board. Boardrooms aren't made that large, so let's consider reducing the board size to 15,000 persons, a 10:1 ratio. To be even more practical, let's cut the board to 1,500 or 500 or 50. Even 50 is a large number, so let's consider a board of 7 or 10. By the time we've dropped to these numbers, any ability of this board to embody the full diversity of its community has been lost several digits ago. Yet the board's ability to be assertive, to be agile, to deliberate, and to speak powerfully on the ownership's behalf increases dramatically as the numbers are reduced. A board of 10 is far more able to take charge of its own leadership obligations than one of 50—or even 20.

In no way are we attempting to suggest or defend any manner of selecting board members that excludes people on the basis of gender, ethnicity, or other such irrelevant characteristic. We are simply acknowledging that (1) the board has to work on behalf of the ownership, (2) groups are more effective at getting anything done well if they are smaller rather than larger, and accordingly that (3) the board's composition cannot perfectly reflect the ownership's diversity. Hence, the board must be the *channel* for diversity rather than pretend it can embody sufficient diversity itself to fulfill its obligation to the ownership.

Acting on the Ownership's Behalf

Let's look now at how a board can be constituted in a way mindful of the diversity among its owners. We assume there to be diversity because the ownership is made up of individuals (or individual organizations, in the case of federations), and there are bound to be differences of opinion. Human beings come in different colors, temperaments, philosophies, appetites, genders, and versions of reality.

With the ownership defined, the board must adopt a frame of mind enabling it to become the channel for its diverse ownership. In other words, boards must act on the owners' behalf and find meaningful ways to connect with them. School board members should deliberate and vote with their best judgment about what ends to demand of the school system on behalf of the general public (owners), not on behalf of parents (customers). This does not mean that the school board is not interested in children or parents, but that their decisions should be made on the basis of community input, not just parental input. Community hospital board members would form their opinions with respect to the ends to be produced on behalf of the community, not on behalf of physicians or administrators.

The board's tough task at this point is to avoid being distracted by other, non-owner voices. Whom the board consults with and how it views the outcome of its consultations are important. It is easy for boards to become captured by one interest group or another. The power elite, the staff, a fiscal officer, or a particularly vociferous stakeholder group can assume control by effectively usurping it from the ownership. But they are not to be heard as owners, lest the true owners be cheated.

Moreover, it is important for the board to recognize that legitimate owners will differ among themselves. The board cannot rest, simply having heard from a vocal part of the legitimate ownership.

Any ownership voice that becomes audible is doubtless the voice of but one segment of ownership. Although the board owes that segment its ear, it owes the silent segments the recognition that one group does not represent all. Elected boards seem particularly vulnerable to the error of listening to segments as if they were the whole, perhaps because these segments are easier to hear (they come to the board) and because elected boards operate in a public spotlight that makes them shrink from the risk of appearing unresponsive.

The board is responsible for ensuring that such corruptions of its obligation to ownership diversity do not occur. So, while the diverse ideas that non-owners bring can be enlightening, stimulating, and perhaps even necessary, hearing them will not satisfy the board's obligation to govern from the ownership's diversity. Equally, listening to just one voice of the ownership does not represent all the voices. Finding and linking to the ownership voices to ensure that more than one voice is heard are the topics of the next section of this CarverGuide.

Linking to the Ownership

To ensure that diverse voices from the ownership are heard, the board should gather data in a way that reflects all aspects of the ownership. The data collection is intended to allow owners' values and wishes to be represented in board debate, largely debate about ends. The statistical base from which the board operates will be rooted in the full diversity of the ownership. The various tides of opinion, the heat and passion with which they are held, and the underlying social issues they reflect will be demonstrated in the data assembled for deliberation.

To collect these data, the board must continually struggle to define and execute the link with its ownership. It should do so with the same vigor it would have if owners were organized and looking over the board's shoulder. However, owners are rarely organized and, in the case of nonprofit organizations, it is even likely that most owners have no idea that they are owners. For this reason, the board cannot be passive in its linkage mechanism. It cannot wait for owners to come forward.

Open meetings, even meetings on cable TV, will not suffice as a means of connecting with owners. People certainly do come to speak to some boards, but they are few and usually come not to voice ownership input but to express customer input. More often than not, it is disgruntled customer input. Disgruntled customers must be attended to, of course, but if it is the board that must do the attending, there is either something awry with management or something misdirected in the message the board sends to customers ("bypass management, bring your problems to us").

In order to connect with the broad band of owners, the board has no choice but to take the initiative, to develop proactive strategies, and to form a bond with owners in innovative ways. The board's commitment to linkage with the ownership can be fulfilled through methods that range from attitudinal to actual. The first, simplest level of commitment is in the board's attitude: board members predicate their board service on the belief that they are the moral trustees for the owners. This commitment establishes a frame of mind that leads the board to appropriate considerations and loyalties when resolving value issues. With this mind-set, the board is less likely to act as if the staff members or very vocal customer groups own the organization. Such a commitment should be codified in governance process policies.

At a second level, the board goes beyond the attitude. It gathers actual evidence of the owners' concerns, needs, and demands. This is not easy to do, but techniques are available. Such techniques include surveys, interviews by third parties, and demographic data. At this level, the board augments its good mind-set by pointedly learning more about who the owners are, what their beliefs are, and what vision they have that is relevant to forming the organization's purpose.

Beyond the informational linkage to owners, the board might develop a more personal connection. In fact, carrying the foregoing techniques to the next level involves actual contact between board members and owners. Board members could conduct structured interviews, focus groups, and public forums. There can be invited presentations by owners or ownership groups at board meetings, and dialogue with other boards or public officials.

No overt action is called for if the board chooses merely to maintain the attitude of ownership linkage. At the next level, using disembodied data to inform the board may require no more than finding the data and studying them. But the personal contact techniques require overt planning and action by board members.

The fact that board members are themselves members of the ownership is a built-in and meaningful, albeit limited, mechanism of linkage. Persons representative of the ownership in color, income level, geographic location, gender, and other characteristics are obviously connected to the ownership as far as those characteristics are concerned. That board members are like many of the owners does prove that specific groups have not been excluded, but it is no proof that they and others are adequately represented. Tokenism might suffice for the former, but only an adequate, ongoing linkage to ownership will ensure the latter.

Specific Ways to Link with Owners and Their Concerns

A board must work diligently to design input processes, commit these methods to policy, and make them part of the board's prescribed governance activity. The aim is not to reach every owner—which would be impossible for large groups—but to reach whatever sampling would be a reasonably representative input. Focus groups and surveys with these persons can be useful. But due to our perennial distortion and negligence of this broad ownership input, it would be healthy to look at each method with a critical eye.

Let's examine a few methods of connecting with the ownership and their concerns. Some methods may not apply to every board, though all will apply to some boards. Boards fully committed to diversity will invent far more than we can list and, indeed, far more than we know.

- Recruiting or appointing new board members can take into account a candidate's ability to identify with and connect to the ownership. This need not mean a slavish formula of board member demographics that turns into a bizarre casting call. So while individually representing a small segment of the ownership is not recommended, firsthand experience with the ownership will help the board member keep focused on ownership issues.

- Whatever its composition, a board can link at least abstractly by attending formally and explicitly to its linkage responsibility. This includes talking about the obligation, ensuring that it receives front-burner consideration, and finding ways to disentangle non-owner (such as staff, funder, or consumer) input from the real thing.

- The board can enhance its linkage ability by gathering statistical data, particularly demographics and values assessments, that relate to the specific ownership as defined. The challenge is getting data about the ownership rather than some other grouping, even though other sources may be less expensive and easier to obtain.

- The board can listen to vocal and assertive subparts of the ownership when these subparts request a hearing, but the board shouldn't assume that these smaller groups represent the total ownership. Try to get such groups to say not only what the organization should produce more of, but also what it should in consequence produce less of. Invite groups that push you in opposite directions to debate the matter among themselves in your presence.

- Owners will have to be helped to understand what questions the board needs answered. We will discuss this issue in the next section. Here, we will remind you that boards should make sure that they don't miseducate the owners. Public boards continually teach the public inappropriate behaviors by the way they structure board meetings and public input. It is as if the public is enticed into missing the point of ownership. While educating the ownership might be a tricky undertaking, in some situations (for example, with smaller trade associations) it is quite achievable. In any event, it must be done as much as possible.

• Written or oral questioning can be used to survey the ownership. Be sure you get a representative sampling, using stratification and randomness as is appropriate. Remember that you are seeking input about what benefits for whom have what relative and absolute worth. You are not seeking input about means.

• Focus groups can sample owners' values and wishes in depth. Notice that the more of these data a public board has, the better it can deal with splinter groups that claim to be representatives of the public. You need not shut them out, but with no ill intent you will drown them out with more extensive data about ownership wishes than they can ever claim.

• Broadcast communication with the ownership if possible, for example, through the commercial press. Report results and delineate ends quandaries. Buy advertising space in a daily newspaper for a quarterly report to the public. Note that this communication is not for the purpose of selling the organization or making it popular—in short, it is not for public relations in the usual sense—but for reporting to the board's "boss." Take great care in the design, since such a report can be terribly boring to owners not nearly as excited about their role as you are.

• The board should establish links with other governing boards. It is likely that the board is only one of several boards that work for the same ownership. A hospital board may have the same ownership as the school system, mental health center, and city council. These boards could be seen as employees working for the same boss. Just as in a management situation, they must communicate productively with each other in order to serve that boss well. A board could create a governance process policy stating: "Since the general public is our ownership, we will contact groups or boards that are part of the general public in order to establish an ends dialogue. Groups will be chosen on the basis of their having (1) knowledge of the issues this board is generally expecting the organization to impact, and/or (2) opposition to the current ends of the organization. Boards will be chosen based on their having (1) a similar or overlapping ownership, or (2) a similar mission. Those boards most capable of communicating about ends and governance process will be given priority."

A board deeply committed to incorporating the diversity of its ownership into the board process will pursue these or even better options for finding and including that diversity. But now we must deal with a critical issue any board faces as it seeks information from the ownership: Just what does the board want to know?

What Information Does the Board Need from Owners?

When boards collect data, what information should they seek? Is there a principle that can be applied to the nature of the input that the board requires? We propose that a board must link with the owners so that the board can represent them well as the board does *its own job*. This means that the board must be careful not to appear to be asking for input about issues already delegated to the CEO. The CEO can get his or her own input—and it will be for entirely different questions.

In Policy Governance, the board establishes ends and executive limitations policies at a broad level of expression, and then charges the CEO to accomplish the ends in any way that works, as long as boundaries formed by the executive limitations policies are not breached. Hence the boundary between board and staff work is very clear and, although the board can change the boundary, the board must not cross it willy-nilly. Good owner input is not obtained by misleading owners to believe that the board is going to make staff decisions.

Clearly, the board requires input about its own decisions, particularly about the ends decisions it must make to direct the organization. Ownership input should be primarily about ends issues, as these are the highest leverage decisions that a board must make on behalf of the owners. Ends decisions answer the question, "What is this organization for?" not "What does it do?" so the input sought should be structured accordingly. Questions such as "Should we

continue to run counseling programs?" or "Should we have bac-
calaureate- or master's-trained staff?" are therefore inappropriate
because these refer to means, not ends.

On the other hand, here are some examples of ends issues that
the board may wish to consult with owners about. Who should be
seen as most in need of safe housing? What level of protection from
fire is worth how much in taxes? Who should be priority recipients
of parenting skills? What educational results for gifted children would
owners give up in return for results for average children? Is achieving
an informed legislature more or less important than a trusted public
image of our membership? In other words, focus the owner discussion
on people's values about what results for whom are worth how much.
The "how much" may be in terms of dollars, relative priority, or other
opportunity cost (such as another result forgone).

When boards interact with other boards, we would suggest that
ends topics remain the focus but that issues of governance methods
also be included. In a community setting, the ends of all community
organizations (political and otherwise) taken together largely define
the effect the community has on people. While boards may not
agree with each other about the aggregate of these separate visions,
it is folly for them to operate in ignorance of them. Yet we do this
routinely. Governance is a natural topic; boards can help each other
find better ways to learn, share diverse opinions, and seek more cre-
ative ways to link with their ownerships.

Connecting with other boards and the ownership gives board
members a wealth of richly diverse wisdom to deliberate in the boardroom. Before moving on to how the board deals with such a range of
feelings and desires, let's look now at one additional source of data.

Adding the Non-Owner Diversity to the Mix

Board diversity is founded in the owners whom it represents. Intro-
ducing that range of diversity into the board process is an obligation
requiring a great deal of commitment and work. But even that will
not be enough. There are other sources of disparate ideas, opinions,

and prognostications with which board members must be acquainted. For it is not enough for the board to govern knowing only as much as the owners. Part of the board's obligation to owners is to study and learn more about the relevant subject matter than owners have time for.

If it were not so, polls could govern quite as well as boards. But while the board must, in a sense, take a poll, in that it must tap the opinions and wishes of the ownership, the board must do more than this. It must take the heterogeneous, conflicting input prevalent in any ownership and then, using its own wisdom, combine ownership input with information and understanding from other sources. This is a difficult, subjective, and often thankless exercise of judgment.

A Texas legislator is reputed to have said, "I vote the way my constituents would vote if they knew what I knew." Boards should take this statement to heart. Proper representation requires knowing what the constituents know, knowing what they cannot be expected to know, and knowing how to blend both with wisdom. The task is difficult but may be made more organized if the board considers several of the following sources of additional knowledge.

Outside experts and advocates. The board can call upon experts to assist in its task. Futurists can stretch a board's thinking about the world for which it will establish ends. Advocacy groups can contribute passion and opposing worldviews of ends worthy of board consideration. Limiting executive means in fiscal and risk policies can be improved by auditors' helping the board know how to recognize fiscal jeopardy.

Trade associations and colleague organizations. Trade associations and organizations in a similar business can provide invaluable assistance to boards. In business, there often exist "industry averages" that allow an organization to compare itself with a whole field. Nonprofit and governmental organizations often have less intelligence available to them than this, but some does exist.

Funders or regulatory bodies. Supraordinate bodies have a stake in your organization and may provide data and opinions from a perspective otherwise hard to find. Inquire about the input that is available.

Staff. A particularly rich and available source of intelligence is the staff itself. The CEO can give the board access to a wide variety of staff member opinions. Do not confuse this input with the traditional staff recommendation wherein the rich diversity of staff input is homogenized into a single party line given to the board.

We are certain that these are not the only classes of wisdom a board might gather. But they suggest an organized approach to the search. See how many good sources your board can identify. Now, with all this confusing information, let's turn to how the board respects and manages dissent at meetings.

Diverse Opinions in the Boardroom

In its efforts to seek out and hear from diverse voices, the board must cultivate an accepting atmosphere about dissent in the boardroom. For diversity to flourish, it should be socially acceptable to examine all ideas, regardless of origin. Otherwise the rich variety of opinion can become either so squelched or so strident as to become ineffective.

It is easy for a board to become so enamored with presenting a united front that it tries to downplay any disagreements. Such a board has forgotten that its real strength is its ability to make decisions from a diverse base. We don't recommend that boards portray to their public a united front in terms of complete agreement, but a united front in terms of forging a powerful single-mindedness from a diverse mix of disagreements.

Useful disagreement occurs without prompting in many boards. In others, members must be given explicit permission, perhaps overt stimulation, to disagree. Board meetings must be made personally safe for diversity. For in the absence of a previously considered and codified process, the dominant characteristic of any confrontation is personality. We may intend our points of departure to be ideas, but interpersonal interaction can easily deteriorate into issues of feelings and control. As alliances are formed and personal power is experienced, the personal source of an idea becomes more important than the idea itself. Not all ideas can prevail, and, if members approach disputes personally, there will be winners and losers. Feeling rebuffed or vindicated may become more important than judging the merit of the idea.

So to ensure that meaningful dissent does not regress into warring personalities, the board needs a process to clarify how dissent is to be expressed. To deal effectively with appropriate diversity, this discussion of process must occur before the specific disagreements arise.

The discussion and the resultant policy help ensure that social rewards operate in support of diversity. Are dissenters looked upon askance? Is it socially safe to disagree? What does the board expect of the chair in pursuing differing viewpoints? The behavioral message must be that disagreement is not only tolerated but is considered necessary to the health of the process.

Furthermore, a board should go outside to seek opposing viewpoints from owners. In other words, board members are not only at their seats to bring their own varying points of view but to see to it that relevant points of view are heard. The board should reach out and bring these other points of view in. The board should be so eager to widen its lens that it imports adversaries to invigorate the process!

Perceived in this way, the board's obligation toward diversity leads to a forum of churning debate, an exciting place, indeed. This debate, of course, must concern the big questions rather than the small ones, the results rather than the methods. The question about diversity then becomes, "Where do we go with all this richness?" It is used chiefly to increase awareness, to decrease smallness, to reveal new ways of looking at the world, and to sharpen the issues. It helps boards pose new, more penetrating questions. The board must make sure the ideas, the points of view, the values get hashed out, listened to, argued, debated, fought over—whatever it takes. Then, the board has to come to some kind of conclusion. All this healthy, provocative discussion and disagreement still must be reduced to a single official position. Diversity is the first step, but it cannot be the last, lest the board bid the organization to ride off in all directions.

The best way to reach this single-voice position is through a carefully constructed process. Disagreement is best resolved from the conceptual top down. In other words, the board should elicit agreement first on the broadest position. For example, it would be much easier to get a majority to support "adequate shelter for home-less persons" than "each person's private space will be at least 120 square feet." The larger the question, the more likely that differ-ences can be resolved.

In Policy Governance, policy development always begins with the broadest application, proceeding into narrower levels one level at a time. It is not that the broadest level is without controversy, but that (1) it must be resolved, in any event, before dealing with sub-sidiary issues, and (2) it probably will be associated with fewer wide swings in value.

Note that this approach requires the board to articulate pol-icy parts. That is, the board does not debate a page of monolithi-cally constructed policy. It debates the very broadest values first, then the next level of issues, then the next. Running all the lev-els together makes wise translation from diversity almost impossi-ble. The process we recommend is only slightly slower, and it is a far more accurate way of turning board values and perspectives into hard copy. Furthermore, policies produced in this highly articulated form are easier to modify later through amendments. Remember that the implications of the various policy alternatives will have been sought, so the board is not simply flying by the seat of its passionately held opinions.

The final step in this policy decision is taking a vote and declar-ing a position. Consensus, if honestly achieved, is certainly work-able, but requiring a consensus before moving on is a prescription for either mediocrity or dishonesty. When the vote is taken, the official pronouncement is as firm as if there had been no disagreement at all. Healthy governance requires that board members agree up front that any position resulting from a fair process is, and of right should be, the position of the board and the only position the CEO cannot ignore.

Consequently, diversity in the boardroom is necessary to good governance, yet bringing the diversity to an official conclusion is necessary for good management. Boards that fail to entertain sufficient diversity in their process cheat the integrity of governance. But boards that fail to save their staffs from that same diversity also cheat the integrity of governance. Staff members will have to deal with diversity, of course, as they carry out the board's wishes. But the diversity they legitimately encounter will be the diversity in themselves and in the world they work in, including the diversity of consumers. If, however, the staff must deal with the board's unsettled diversity, the board has not done its job. It should not be up to staff members to answer to factions and dissenting voices on the board.

The board's agreement on its process of bringing wide diversity to an official board position is embodied as a policy in the governance process category. Individual freedom of opinion, however, need not be sacrificed. There is no reason that the members of a board should pretend they agree on content after the vote when they did not before. But they must support the validity of the decision that was made, as well as the procedural integrity used, and rigorously refrain from undermining the decision arrived at by the board. Supporting the process only when you win the vote is not supporting the process.

Split votes are to be expected. In fact, recurring unanimous votes are suspect. All persons on a board may, on a given issue, agree. But if the voting record of a board is regularly or predominantly one of unanimous votes, we must question whether dissent is being squelched or if the issues are simply not important enough to disagree about. Either possibility calls for an examination of board process.

Summary

Diversity in the boardroom is not an option, nor is it a reaction to political correctness. Diversity on behalf of—and founded in—the ownership is the only morally defensible foundation for a board setting about its task. Let us conclude the matter with a list that summarizes our rationale and provides examples of the considerations raised at each step.

Rationale	*Questions to Address*
• There are persons or populations who either legally or morally own the organization.	Who are these owners? Are they easy to describe or difficult (could be either)? Are they easy to identify and find personally? Can the board readily distinguish owners from customers and other stakeholders?
• These persons or populations are never homogeneous but are diverse in many respects.	What is the nature of their diversity? Are these simply different points of view, or deep, cultural rifts among subparts of the ownership?
• The board's moral authority arises from its representation of these owners.	How can the board distinguish this moral imperative from the more mechanical authority given by nonprofit statutes or enabling legislation?
• Proper representation of owners means including the owners' range of diversity in the board.	How can board members represent the range? Will "constituent" board members help or hurt the commitment to represent a range? If constituent members are used, what do we do about all the constituencies not covered?

Rationale	*Questions to Address*
• There are ascending levels of governance integrity with respect to honoring that diversity.	How much integrity can we begin with? Over what period of time can we develop ourselves to higher levels? What strategies to reach out can we develop? What are the right questions to ask owners who are also customers so that they give true owner input?
• From the foundation of diversity, the board can integrate even more diversity from experts or others.	Are we reaching out to enough resources? Do we know what resources exist? How clear are we about what to ask of them? How can we be certain to use expert help to inform our wisdom rather than to substitute for it?
• From this rich base, a board can deal with diversity in ways that support individuals in their dissent.	How safe is it in our board to dissent? When no dissent is expressed, do we move on, or do we inquire about the absence of dissent? If dissent is expressed only by one person, do we see that person as a problem?
• Despite the wide range of diversity, the board must come to a conclusion that gives the organization a unified direction.	How much debate is enough? How do we know when to stop? Have we agreed on how we'll look at split votes? Do we expect we will all agree? Are we committed to supporting the integrity of governance even when we lose the vote?
• The CEO is beholden to the board's unified direction, not to its diversity.	Does the CEO know to treat any board decision as if it were unanimous? Do board members own the problem of diversity, rather than letting unresolved diversity impinge upon the CEO and staff?

The CarverGuide
Series on Effective
Board Governance

The Policy Governance model was created by John Carver in the mid-1970s as a radical alternative to the conventional wisdom about how governance should proceed. All governance literature at that time—as virtually all of it is even today—was based on ideas about the board's role and responsibilities that had been around for a very long time.

Boards convinced that Policy Governance offers a breakthrough in governance thinking encounter a confusing problem: most printed matter and training reinforce old governance ideas rather than the new ones. It is not that widely available sources do not have wisdom to offer. Indeed, they do. But the wisdom they have is rooted in traditional governance ideas. One of the great difficulties of a paradigm shift is that perfectly fine wisdom in a previous paradigm can become poor judgment in a new one. The person most expert in flying a propeller-driven plane is not, therefore, expert in piloting a jet.

Consequently, most current guides and training materials can actually handicap boards trying to use the new governance ideas in Policy Governance. The CarverGuide series was created to remedy this situation. The series offers detailed guidance on specific board responsibilities and operations based on the *new* paradigm rather than the traditional approach.

The first CarverGuide in the series presented an overview of the fundamental principles of the Policy Governance model. As a model, Policy Governance is designed to embrace all further issues of governance that are specific to different organizations and different circumstances. That is, it is not specifically about fiscal oversight, CEO evaluation, planning, agenda control, committee operation, or the other many facets of board leadership. It is, in fact, about all of them. It is a basic set of concepts and principles that lay the groundwork for determining appropriate board leadership about these and other common governance issues. Nonetheless, many boards need specific materials that individually do address these different facets of board leadership.

Having presented the overview in the first CarverGuide, we deal with the various areas of board concern one at a time in the succeeding guides in this series. It is our hope that the concepts and recommendations we present in this series will help all boards achieve a powerful overhaul of their approach to governance. Indeed, the practices we recommend in the CarverGuide Series really make sense only as parts of the larger picture of board leadership held up by the Policy Governance model.